Give a little love to a child,
and you get a great deal back.

John Ruskin

Other books in the *"Language of"* Series...

Blue Mountain Arts®

It's Great to Have a Brother like You

It's Great to Have a Sister like You

The Language of Brides

The Language of Courage and Inner Strength

The Language of Friendship

The Language of Happiness

The Language of Love

The Language of Marriage

The Language of Positive Thinking

The Language of Prayer

The Language of Recovery

The Language of Success

The Language of Teaching

The Language of Teenagers

Thoughts to Share with a Wonderful Daughter

Thoughts to Share with a Wonderful Father

Thoughts to Share with a Wonderful Mother

Thoughts to Share with a Wonderful Son

You Will Always Have an Angel Watching Over You

The Language of

PARENTING

*A Blue Mountain Arts® Collection
on the Joys of Being a Parent*

Blue Mountain Press™

SPS Studios, Inc., Boulder, Colorado

The publisher wishes to acknowledge and thank Marge Hansen for her help in compiling the poems and quotations in this collection.

Library of Congress Catalog Card Number: 2001000230
ISBN: 0-88396-587-9

We wish to thank Susan Polis Schutz for permission to reprint the following poems that appear in this publication: "The love of a family...," "What Is a Daughter?," "For a New Parent," "What Is a Son?," and "It is often difficult...." Copyright © 1980, 1991, 1992, 1993, 2001 by Stephen Schutz and Susan Polis Schutz. All rights reserved.

ACKNOWLEDGMENTS appear on page 48.

Certain trademarks are used under license.

Manufactured in Thailand
First Printing: March 2001

This book is printed on recycled paper.

Library of Congress Cataloging-in-Publication Data

The language of parenting : a Blue Mountain Arts collection on the joys of being a parent.
    p.   cm. — (The "Language of" Series...)
  ISBN 0-88396-587-9 (alk. paper)
  1. Child rearing—Quotations, maxims, etc. 2. Parenting—Quotations, maxims, etc. 3. Child rearing—Poetry. 4. Parenting—Poetry. I. SPS Studios (Firm) II. Series.
  PN6084.C48 L36 2001
  649'.1—dc21

2001000230
CIP

SPS Studios, Inc.

P.O. Box 4549, Boulder, Colorado 80306

Contents

(Authors listed in order of first appearance)

It is beautiful to see
in how many lives
the joy and love of a child
has brought unity and peace!

Mother Teresa of Calcutta

Life is a flame that is always burning itself out,
but it catches fire again every time a child is born.

George Bernard Shaw

To have a child
is to be given
the world to hold
in your hands...

And the entire universe
to try to fit
inside your heart.

Douglas Pagels

Being a Parent
Is a Special Gift

Being a parent
is such a wonderful thing.
It's a joy beyond compare,
a happiness no words can describe.
As you guide your child
through the problems of life,
and offer the encouragement
needed to achieve so many things,
you will need an abundance
of patience, kindness,
and understanding,
but everything you give
will be returned tenfold
in love and appreciation.
Being a parent is a special gift
that blesses your life
with happiness, love,
and a lifetime of memories.

— Deanne Laura Gilbert

What Parents Are
to Their Children

A place they can search for comfort.
Eyes they can look at and trust.
A hand they can reach out and clasp.
A heart that understands and doesn't judge.

Someone they can lean on and learn from.
A source of wisdom and loving advice.
A million memories in the making.
A precious companion on the path of life.

A door that is always open.
A caring, gentle hug.
A time that is devoted to family alone.
A reflection of love.

L. N. Mallory

Taking care of their children, seeing them grow
and develop into fine people, gives most parents…
their greatest satisfaction in life.

Benjamin Spock, M.D., and Michael B. Rothenberg, M.D.

Fifty years from now, it will not matter
what kind of car you drove,
what kind of house you lived in,
how much you had in your bank account,
or what your clothes looked like.
But the world may be a little better because
you were important in the life of a child.

»})» Anonymous

Raising healthy children is the most important work of the culture.
If you have children, parenting is your most important job. What you do
when your children are small will contribute to the pain or the joy of the
rest of your life. Little other work has such far-reaching effects,
influencing present and future generations alike.

»})» Dr. Louise Hart

We find a delight in the beauty and happiness of
children that makes the heart too big for the body.

»})» Ralph Waldo Emerson

As You Enter the
Awesome Role of Parenthood

As a parent, you have been blessed with the greatest gift this world has to offer. This child has been given into your care to love and to help grow. Do not hold expectations on your child; he may not be equipped to meet them. Do not demand that this child see the world through your eyes. Be always mindful that although guidance is necessary, this child has the right to be an individual.

Love and guidance are the only gifts you can give your child. Do not attempt to break the spirit of a strong-willed child, rather curb it gently to conform to the demands of society and steer him continually in the right direction, while always allowing him the space required to blossom into that beautiful person he is destined to be. Do not scorn the shy or quiet child. He is a special person deep inside. He will open up to love and friendship as he feels comfortable. Always encourage him in word and example. Never desire that your child be what he isn't.

Remember that it is you who chose to embark on this most difficult but enormously rewarding role as parent. Enjoy your child for who he is. Guide him and, above all, offer love and support in endless quantities.

Karen M. Talmo

For all parents, the birth of a child means that life will never be the same again, and each new child forces changes and reorderings of old relationships. Our pleasures and pains are now bound up in yet another's life, another's needs, experiences, feelings, triumphs, and misfortunes, and bound more closely than they may ever have been before.

 Fred Rogers

Accept your children as perfect, as whole, and treat them as though they already are what they can become. Send them messages all the time that they are great.... Give them no judgments or negative reinforcement for not pleasing you; simply love them for what they are, and treat them as though they already are what they can become. This combination allows them to take control of their lives and keeps them feeling positive about themselves in each moment that they are here. It gives them goals to shoot for, but it gives them unconditional love and acceptance of wherever they are in the pursuit of any goals they might have for themselves. Believe it or not, they have much more to teach you about living fully in the present than you have to teach them. You may very well have lost your childlike fascination for the miracle that life is, but if you watch them — stop treating them as apprentice people who are on their way to being somebody, and instead enjoy them for where they are — the rest of it will all fall into place naturally.

Dr. Wayne W. Dyer

The earlier someone is taught how to live in the most effortless, harmonious, and creative way, the more likely it is that all of life will bring success. This is what we are asked to pass on to our children, and if we can do it, nothing brings more joy and pride.

Deepak Chopra, M.D.

For a New Parent

Your baby is
a beautiful, innocent, tiny person
who will depend on you for everything
Play with your baby
Teach your baby
all you know
Protect your baby
from all possible hurt
Love your baby at all times
Give your baby
stability and family support

Your baby will give you
the deepest understanding of happiness
Your baby is
a beautiful miracle
of love and life

                                Susan Polis Schutz

There is a certain beauty in the world
 when a new life enters it,
 just as there is beauty
 in the blossoming of a new parent.

                         Amy Michele Shockey

Some Advice to New Parents
(from a Baby's Viewpoint)

"Our first year together will be fleeting.
There will be moments that become memories
to cherish in our minds, our hearts,
and our scrapbooks.
We will grasp at images
and hold them for only wisps of time.

I'll change so quickly.
You'll grow as much as I do, and in as many ways.
The trying, crying times are but moments, too.
They will pass and, in passing, will make memories
that are as wonderful to hold as I am now.

Trust yourself, for God chose you to be my parents,
knowing that you will love me, care for me, and know me
as no one else ever will."

Linda Ferree

A child may be as new to the world as snowdrops in January, and
yet already have a good and keen and deep understanding, a full mind
and a hospitable heart. He may be able to think hard, imagine richly,
face trouble, take good care of himself and of others, keep well, and
live abundantly.

Walter de la Mare

Gifts from Parents to Children

Time is the most valuable gift we can give our kids — or anyone. Money and things are soon gone. But memories and feelings of love can last a lifetime. Care about kids enough to spend time with them.

Glen C. Griffin, M.D.

The gift of time, gentle communication with love and caring in your hearts, a genuine interest in your child, and a belief in his ability to be bright and interesting are powerful ways to love a child!

Bobbie Sandoz

It must have been an unusually clear and beautiful night for someone to have said, "Let's wake the baby and show her the stars." The night sky, the constant rolling of breakers against the shore, the stupendous light of the stars, all made an indelible impression on me. I was intuitively aware not only of a beauty I had never seen before but also that the world was far greater than the protected limits of the small child's world which was all that I had known thus far. I had a total, if not very conscious, moment of revelation; I saw creation bursting the bounds of daily restriction, and stretching out from dimension to dimension, beyond any human comprehension.

 Madeleine L'Engle

A happy childhood is one of the best gifts that parents have it in their power to bestow.

Mary Cholmondeley

One of the greatest gifts we can give our children is a sense of mastery, of being able to do something very well. Such a special competence gives a big boost to one's self-esteem…. No matter how far removed a child's expertise is from your own areas of interest, you should treat it with interest, respect, and admiration.

Charles Schaefer, Ph.D.

There are only two lasting bequests we can give our children. One is roots, the other wings.

Hodding Carter

Unconditional love
is the greatest gift
any parent could ever give.

Dena Dilaconi

Gifts from Children to Parents

Children provide parents with a second chance to dream and wonder. They, in all innocence and wide-eyed belief, pull us out of our ho-hum reality into the world as they see it. And often what they reveal to us is more real and alive than what we offer them. Was my opinion of dandelions more valid than that of my older son who, from the time he was allowed to toddle outdoors, spent most of the springtime gathering huge bouquets of the weed? He forever changed me. I see their color now and understand the joy he had in their discovery. Each spring gives me the chance anew to remember a little yellow-nosed boy eagerly offering me his treasure: "These are for you, Mom."

Ellen Walker

All parents expect to influence their children, but many are surprised to find that it's a two-way street and that they learn and gain from their parenting and their children. In other words, parenting is an enormously influential developmental step for adults in their own lives.

Benjamin Spock, M.D., and Michael B. Rothenberg, M.D.

Grown-ups never understand anything for themselves, and it is tiresome for children to be always and forever explaining things to them.

Antoine de Saint-Exupéry

Parents lend children their experience and a vicarious memory; children endow their parents with a vicarious immortality.

George Santayana

Children are adoring, of parents in particular. All figures of religious and secular power are nothing in a child's eyes when compared to a parent. If the Chair of the Board felt about you the way your child does, you would be president of the company tomorrow. Caution, such power has consequences. Use it responsibly.

Bob Keeshan
(Captain Kangaroo)

A Small Child

No business success,
No personal achievement,
Is half as rewarding
As when a small child
Climbs into your lap
And goes to sleep
In perfect peace,
Confident in your love.

Tom Ryan

Teaching the Children

Parents are in many ways like teachers, perhaps even more so, for they are the teachers of a lifetime.

Simon Glustrom

Children are naturally curious, but it's lots of work to be the teacher, parent, or sibling of a child who's always asking questions, always taking things apart, always making a mess. But curiosity is an important part of being successful because that is what drives someone to think a little harder, do a little more.

Karin Ireland

You cannot teach a child to take care of himself unless you will let him take care of himself. He will make mistakes, and out of these mistakes will come his wisdom.

Henry Ward Beecher

To learn with one's children the lesson of starting life honestly, with the powers, capacities, tendencies which one has, seems to me the primary law of parenthood.

Henry Noble MacCracken

Kids love to feel smart and those who do are the ones who succeed. Kids have a natural enthusiasm for learning and talking about what they learn and when they do, they learn even more.

Karin Ireland

As [children] are given by God, we
    so must have them and love them;
Teach them as best we can, and
    let each of them follow his nature.
One will have talents of one sort,
    and different talents another.
Every one uses his own, in his
    own individual fashion.

Johann Wolfgang von Goethe

To know how to suggest is the art of teaching.

Henri Frédéric Amiel

We learn only from those we love.

Johann Wolfgang von Goethe

Children Learn from What They See

Remember that children mainly learn from what you are, not what you say. Your own practice is always the greatest positive influence. Children need you as a model and example; in that sense, watching you is their practice from very early on. If they see you growing and changing and finding more meaning and joy in your own life, the expression "being in harmony with the universe" takes on practical force. They will want that for themselves, even if they don't yet grasp the principles involved.

Deepak Chopra, M.D.

Role modeling is the most basic responsibility of parents. They are handing life's scripts to their children, scripts that in all likelihood will be acted out for much of the rest of the children's lives.

Stephen R. Covey

Children watch the way their parents live their lives. If they like what they see, if it makes sense to them, they will live their lives that way, too.

Colin Powell

To Give a Child a Dream

You cannot practice for her every day
The knowledge that you give her will not stream
On her young mind in one bright, blinding ray
But you can plant a dream

Ah, you can plant a dream in her young heart
A dream of excellence whose light will gleam
Upon her pathway as the years depart
Your words can plant a dream

To sow a dream and see it spread and grow
To light a lamp and watch its brightness gleam
Here is a gift that is divine I know
To give a child a dream

Anne Campbell

Give them nature. Let their souls drink in all that is pure and sweet. Rear them, if possible, amid pleasant surroundings…. Let nature teach them the lessons of good and proper living…. Put the best in them in contact with the best outside. They will absorb it as a plant does sunshine and dew.

Luther Burbank

Know you what it is to be a child?... It is to... believe in love, to believe in loveliness, to believe in belief; it is to be so little that the elves can reach to whisper in your ear; it is to turn pumpkins into coaches and mice into horses, lowness into loftiness and nothing into everything, for each child has its fairy godmother in its soul.

Francis Thompson

Between the dark and the daylight,
When the night is beginning to lower,
Comes a pause in the day's occupations,
That is known as the Children's Hour.

Henry Wadsworth Longfellow

Parents bear the first and primary responsibility for their sons and daughters — to feed them, to sing them to sleep, to teach them to ride a bike, to encourage their talents, to help them develop spiritual lives, to make countless daily decisions that determine whom they have the potential to become.

Hillary Rodham Clinton

What Is a Son?

A son is
a kite flying through
    the trees
a tadpole turning into a frog
a dandelion in the wind

A son is
a mischievous smile
laughing eyes
a scrape on the knees

A son is a wonder
an excitement
a burst of energy
an animation
a spirited breeze
A son is everything
    wonderful
A son is love

Susan Polis Schutz

What Is a Daughter?

A daughter is
a rainbow bubble
a star glimmering in the sky
a rosebud after a storm
a caterpillar turning into a butterfly

A daughter is
hair flying in the wind
red cheeks that glisten in
    the sunshine
big daydream eyes

A daughter is
a wonder
a sweetness, a secret, an artist
a perception, a delight

A daughter is
everything beautiful
A daughter is
love

Susan Polis Schutz

Children Are...

...miracles that never cease to be miraculous....
full of beauty and forever beautiful.... loving
and caring and truly amazing.

— Deanna Beisser

...touches that bond you for life, smiles that
make your heart soar... and love that goes
so deep it becomes part of your soul.

— Barbara Cage

...gifts from God. Appreciate them, be glad they are a part
of your life, and recognize the honor and miracle that has
been bestowed upon you. If you know a child, you are
blessed. They are radiant, tender beings of light. They may
be expensive, but when you nurture the soul of a child, you
are gaining heavenly riches.

— Judy Ford

Children Are Angels Who Walk the Earth

When angels walk the earth,
they leave their wings behind.
With innocence they join us and take on earthly souls.
But you can find them staring longingly at fluttering butterflies,
climbing to the heights of treetops,
or hanging from a basketball hoop.
Can these be signs that they're missing the wings
that once carried them above?

They give themselves away
in toothless smiles, skinned-knee teardrops, and peanut-butter kisses.
These wingless little miracles can't hide for very long.
Their secret is revealed in counted blessings
while cradled in your arms.

You'll never quite explain how your heart soars at off-key recitals
or the bursting pride you hold for a masterpiece created in fingerpaint,
not to mention the unbridled need to hang it on your fridge.
You needn't question the love you hold
for funny faces or knock-knock jokes.

For the path of these angels who walk the earth
travels straight into your heart,
and your life will be devoted
to giving their dreams wings to fly.

Linda LaBella-Morgan

Being a Parent Is...

...a complex thing. It involves not only trying to feel what our children are feeling and trying to know just how much to do to help them with what they cannot yet do for themselves, but also trying to know how much *not* to do. We must also learn to recognize our children's real capacities and respect their need to do things for themselves.

Fred Rogers

...not a natural ability all of us are born with. It is a learning process that takes time, patience, and the development of skills.

Charles Schaefer, Ph.D.

...the pride and love you feel
the moment you first hold
your child in your arms.

Deanne Laura Gilbert

...always giving of yourself for your children... spending time with them no matter how tired you feel... listening and understanding... and always making them feel secure, happy, and loved.

Donna Gephart

...wanting to keep your children from all hurt and harm, but knowing that they must be taught to take care of themselves.

Karen Kolpien-Bugaj

...a blessing. Together you and your child are carving a life; by helping your child grow into a beautiful human being, you are giving something of immense value to humanity and all of us are enriched.

Judy Ford

Parenting Can Be Hard Sometimes

The greatest parenting challenge lies in being responsible for guiding, teaching, and urging your child toward his best self — which includes the need to notice his mistakes and help him correct them — while simultaneously accepting and loving him as he exists now, before his faults are rectified.

Bobbie Sandoz

Nobody's family can hang out the sign: "Nothing the Matter Here."

Chinese Proverb

Parenting is hard, but children are a joy. When you love a child, it changes you! You have a new focus. When you become a mother or father, you have a new role and a new responsibility. Fortunately parenting is a two-way street — you walk together, and as you take them by the hand, they take you by the heart. You give to them and they give to you. And although parenting is demanding, intriguing, frustrating, frightening, and confusing, children are joyful, entertaining, enlightening, and heartwarming. We show them the ways of the world, and they show us the ways of the heart.

Judy Ford

Even though being a parent will never be easy, remember that you have the most important job in the world. Trust your own judgment, and you will do just fine. Ask for help when you need it, take time out for laughter and tears, and trust that experience will ease some of your fears. As a parent, you are shaping the future.

— Jacqueline Schiff

Before I got married I had six theories about bringing up children; now I have six children and no theories.

— John Wilmot

How can you explain that having a child drives you as far apart as you've ever been, yet it draws you together more deeply and magically than ever before — all at the same time?

That after you've both spent an aggravating, mind-numbing hour and a half rocking, walking, patting, *begging* your child to sleep, there's nothing you'd rather do than spend the next hour and a half together, watching this angel sleep.

— Paul Reiser

You Are Not Alone

There are times as a parent you feel entirely alone, helpless, with nowhere to turn. You are not alone. Parents all over the world, in every country, society, and all facets of life feel this same way.

During these times, it may help to remember that your child is also feeling helpless and may be reaching out for a helping hand. Know that no child is inherently bad and that with love and support, you will both survive the most difficult of times. Be that helping hand for your child, help him work through his problems or his troubled times. Let him know you care and that you are always there for him. Help him to realize that even though it seems as if nothing will ever be right again, with hope, faith, determination, and love, things will eventually turn around. Share with him your wisdom in having lived through childhood. Try to remember how important and devastating the simplest of situations can be for a child. Don't make light of his very real feelings; understand them and help him through.

The role of parent is the hardest job you will ever encounter, but it is also the most rewarding and fulfilling. As you teach your child to have hope, faith, determination, and love, summon up those same emotions within yourself, and persevere. You will never be sorry you did.

Karen M. Talmo

Some parents bring up their children on thunder and lightning, but thunder and lightning never yet made anything grow. Rain or sunshine cause growth — quiet, penetrating forces that develop life.

Author Unknown

The primary key to successful parenting lies in knowing how to combine love with discipline and fulfilling these two goals of parenting simultaneously! In order to accomplish this, you must learn to love and accept your child in the very moment he's crying, making a mistake, or misbehaving. You must also control and discipline him as needed, no matter how tenderly you're feeling toward him or how much you prefer to have only peaceful, happy times together. In this way, you encircle both loving and correcting, bring these two opposites together, and execute them in the same moment. This merging of love with discipline enables you to both nurture and guide your child with balance at all times.

Bobbie Sandoz

Words to Tell Your Children When They're Older

I loved you enough to ask where you were going, with whom, and what time you would be home.

I loved you enough to be silent and let you discover that your new best friend was a creep.

I loved you enough to stand over you for two hours while you cleaned your room — a job that would have taken me fifteen minutes.

I loved you enough to let you assume responsibility for your actions even when the penalties were so harsh they almost broke my heart.

But most of all, I loved you enough to say "no" when I knew you would hate me for it. Those were the most difficult battles of them all. I'm glad I won them, because in the end you won something, too.

Author Unknown

Encourage Your Children...

The root meaning of the word *encouragement* is *to give heart*. When we encourage our children, we give them courage from our hearts to theirs. It is our job to help and support them while they develop the skills and confidence they need to stand on their own. This can be a very delicate matter: Knowing when to step in and when to step aside, when to praise and when to offer constructive criticism is an art, not a science.

Dorothy Law Nolte and Rachel Harris

Children need encouragement, just as plants need water. They cannot survive without it.

Rudolph Dreikurs

Five Keys to Using Encouragement to Create Higher Self-Esteem in Your Children

1. Build on your children's strengths by catching them doing something right.
2. Express appreciation when your children are cooperative and helpful.
3. Give positive support for each step along the way to achieving a goal or new behavior.
4. Show confidence.
5. Nurture success.

Stephanie Marston

...and Their Creativity

Children raised in such a way as to encourage natural creativity are children encouraged to be their own selves, to feel free not to fit in or not to live life only as others do. They are brought up to understand that it is impossible to be just like everyone else and still have anything to offer. They learn very early that conforming and adjusting to life are not worthwhile goals, and that it is all right to challenge established authority, to ask why, and to try new ways of doing things....

Creative children are unafraid of their own greatness. They are encouraged to think of themselves in ways which are never limiting. They are not taught to believe in heroes or to make other people more significant than themselves. Creativity and risking go hand in hand. Children need to know from the very beginning that they have genius and greatness residing within them, and that they can choose to allow those qualities to flourish.

Dr. Wayne W. Dyer

To be a good parent you need to genuinely like children and enjoy being around them. This means you have to be in touch with the childlike spirit that exists in all of us. This spirit is full of wonder, enthusiasm, imagination, curiosity, and spontaneity.

Charles Schaefer, Ph.D.

Babies do not want to hear about babies; they like to be told of giants and castles.

Samuel Johnson

Sing, Dance, and Have Fun Together

A nurturing home is a place where parents and children can relax and unwind from the pressures of the day. Laughing, singing, and dancing are the fastest ways to transform worries into celebration. Having fun together will strengthen your family and foster easy, honest relationships among all of you. And as your children grow they are much more likely to enjoy being with the family if everyone is having a good time....

Laughter serves as a bridge between you and your child, bringing you closer. Laugh often; tell little jokes without poking fun or teasing. Look at the humorous side of life. When laughter and music are common threads running through your encounters with your child, family life is more exciting, and precious memories are made. Have a song in your heart. Be free with your laughter, spontaneous with your dance, and your children will think of you with a twinkle in their eye.

Judy Ford

In every place where humans toil, in every dream and plan,
The laughter of the children shapes the destiny of man.

Edgar A. Guest

Kids are a great excuse to be silly.... Seek out and share natural highs with your family — adventures, art, making music, cuddling, laughter, excitement. Look for beautiful sunsets and rainbows. Share the amazement, the awe, with each other....

Start to play today. Look for things that tickle your funny bone. Put down this book and do one fun thing you love to do. Right now. You deserve joy in your life; it's never too late to have a happy childhood! Make fun time a high priority in your family. Set aside a half day to play together. Go for a walk or a bike ride. Go to the museum or the zoo. Be silly with your kids at least once a day.

Dr. Louise Hart

Obviously, it would be ludicrous to suggest that parents sit around laughing merrily through the shattered glasses, misplaced retainers, peanut-butter prints on the new wallpaper, and chocolate syrup on the rug. But most of us agree that a sense of humor is a very good quality. In fact, we all want our children to acquire a sense of humor. So when something is truly funny and no real damage has been done, the best response may be the most obvious — just laugh.

Nancy Samalin

Make Each Day
with Your Child Special

Do not underestimate the importance of the seemingly routine, because each day is a special occasion to your child. You constantly shape the memories that he will carry for the rest of his life, and most of the time you are unaware that you are doing it. Yet one day when he is home from college he will tell you, much to your surprise, how important it was to him that you always fixed him popcorn in that big yellow bowl.

Craig Chappelow

Hold them, touch them, kiss them, be physical with them. They will learn to love themselves if they feel loved by you, and they cannot get that feeling of being attractive unless they actually experience it with you, the most important person in their young lives.... Being touched and held by a parent is crucial in the development of a young child's self-image. They need to feel loved, really loved a lot, in their young lives. They need to feel beautiful, important, attractive, and wanted.... I say tell them that you love them every day. And even more important, show them that they are lovable by grabbing them, hugging them, kissing them, and demonstrating that they are really terrific. The more you do it, the more you are sending them wonderfully important messages about their own value, and soon they will love themselves as you love them, and that is our goal after all.

Dr. Wayne W. Dyer

Fill Your Child's World
with Kindness and Love

Each time we sensitize our children to looking at the world and listening to it from their hearts while joining us in acts of caring and kindness, true urges to love, care, and share will develop from deep within them.

We can further teach our children that our internal feelings and attitudes as well as our behaviors are magnets which draw similar people and experiences to us. Thus, if we're judgmental and attacking, we'll find ourselves dealing with the judgments of others. If our hearts are filled with love and appreciation, we'll find ourselves surrounded by loving friends and heartfelt experiences.

Bobbie Sandoz

I think that I would rather teach a child
The joys of kindness than long hours to spend
Poring o'er multiple and dividend;
How differing natures may be reconciled
Rather than just how cost accounts are filed;
How to live bravely to its end
Rather than how one fortress to defend,
Or how gold coins once gathered can be piled.

There is an education of the mind
Which all require and parents early start,
But there is training of a nobler kind
And that's the education of the heart.
Lessons that are most difficult to give
Are faith and courage and the way to live.

Edgar A. Guest

The Importance of Family

Childhood is a time when the foundations for life are laid by our parents. So today holds the key to the future.

Creating peace in the world starts with creating peace in our families. It's up to us to provide the richest environment possible so that our children can grow up to express their fullest humanity. What more rewarding responsibility could you have than to raise a generation of loving, compassionate, responsible, caring, productive adults? When I think about the possibility of a world filled with this sort of nurturing individual, I am filled with hope and awe.

Stephanie Marston

The only rock I know that stays steady, the only institution I know that works, is the family. I was brought up to believe in it — and I do. Because I think a civilized world can't remain civilized for long if its foundation is built on anything but the family. A city, state, or country can't be any more than the sum of its vital parts — millions of family units.... It all starts at home.

Lee Iacocca

In reality, families — forged as much in love and experience as in biology — come in all forms and configurations.

Yet, one thing about families remains unchanging and constant.

In family, children grow and learn how to be the adults they will eventually become by modeling themselves after the adults in their lives.

Wayne Dosick

The family is one of
nature's masterpieces.
George Santayana

The family is the nucleus
of civilization.
Will Durant

The love
of a family
is so
uplifting

The warmth
of a family
is so
comforting

The support
of a family
is so reassuring

The attitude
of a family
towards
each other
molds one's
attitude forever
towards the
world
Susan Polis Schutz

On Being a Mother...

The love between a mother and her child is a bond of the strongest kind. It is a love of the present, interwoven with memories of the past and dreams of the future. It is an unconditional, forever kind of love.

Barbara Cage

It is often difficult, tiresome and hard to be a mother, and there is never a rest from being a mother, but helping my children grow to be competent, caring, sensitive, successful, happy individuals is the most important thing I could ever do, and it is, by far, the most loving and rewarding.

Susan Polis Schutz

The mother's heart is the child's schoolroom.

Henry Ward Beecher

On Being a Father...

A father is a guide on the journey to adulthood, a teacher of morals and values. He listens to problems and helps to find their solutions. He is a friend, always there to share the good and the bad. He is someone who gets respect because he deserves it, trust because he earns it, and love because of all he is.

M. Joye

A little child, a limber elf,
Singing, dancing to itself,
A fairy thing with red, round cheeks,
That always finds, and never seeks,
Makes such a vision to the sight
As fills a father's eyes with light.

Samuel Taylor Coleridge

Blessed indeed is the man who hears many gentle voices call him father!

Lydia M. Child

More than Anything Else, Children Need Love

Conveying our love to our children is priority number one. It needs to come before any other aspect of the parenting process. Kids don't care how much you know until they know how much you care. Before you offer correction, guidance, or suggestions, your unconditional love needs to be the basis of your relationship with your children.

Stephanie Marston

Take this still very young one into the soft understanding of your heart and patiently bathe it in love. Have confidence in your child, even though your child may have little in himself, and resolve to remain a constant friend... one who can be turned to, one who will support and never judge, and one who emanates hope by a quiet knowing of how it will all turn out.

Hugh Prather

Give a little love to a child, and you get a great deal back.

John Ruskin

The Nine Basic Ingredients
for Falling in Love with Your Kids:

1. Spend time together.
2. Develop common interests.
3. Play together.
4. Talk together.
5. Touch each other.
6. Tell your children often that you love them.
7. Treat your kids as if they are the most important people in the world.
8. Create lasting memories.
9. Celebrate their uniqueness.

Stephanie Marston

Some people think of love as meaning simply the expression of physical and emotional affection. Parental love has more sides than that. It's wanting the children to grow up to be responsible citizens and successful individuals. It's reminding them every day, if only in the kindliest manner, how to behave to become that kind of person.

There are many other aspects to managing and motivating children.... But the parents' love for their children and the responding love of their children for them is by far the most important.

Benjamin Spock, M.D.

The Things You Want
Them to Remember...

Before I leave this world,
I want to tell my children
a few very important things
about who I am
and what I believe.
It may not make a difference
in the big scheme of things,
but at least for me,
I will feel as if
I shared my heart
and the truths of my soul.
I want them to know that my spirit
danced with each new day
and quietly kissed each evening good-night,
that I loved them with all that I am,
and that wherever their journeys lead them,
my love will be there, too.

— Deanna Beisser

Too Soon the Children Grow

The time goes by so quickly ~ Precious moments need to be shared while they can ~ The lives of children move on so swiftly, and there are so many days that are already memories ~ Of all the things I have come to understand, the best is to cherish today — before it's too late ~ Don't worry about things that don't matter ~ The chores can always get done some other time ~ Do what you must, but do what it takes... to make the sunlight shine ~

I know I've got other things to do ~ There are people to talk with, things to straighten up, problems to work out, and places to go ~ But today, they'll all have to wait ~ Far more important things are on my mind ~ A child I love ranks above everything else ~ And sometimes the most beautiful and most important thing we can do is just be together with the ones we love... and make the sunlight shine ~

Ceal Carson

I see that twinkle in your eye
And know some mischief you might try.
I'll watch you grow just like the moon
From slip to fullness, all too soon.

Gilson

Parents' Creed

And a woman who held a babe against her bosom said, Speak to us of Children. And he said: Your children are not your children. They are the sons and daughters of Life's longing for itself. They come through you but not from you, and though they are with you yet they belong not to you. You may give them your love but not your thoughts, for they have their own thoughts. You may house their bodies but not their souls, for their souls dwell in the house of tomorrow, which you cannot visit, not even in your dreams. You may strive to be like them, but seek not to make them like you. For life goes not backward nor tarries with yesterday. You are the bows from which your children as living arrows are sent forth.

Kahlil Gibran

They must go free
Like fishes in the sea
Or starlings in the skies
Whilst you remain
The shore where casually they
Come again.

Frances Crofts Cornford

Always Cherish the Joys of Being a Parent

Hold close to your heart
the moments when tiny fingers
reach out to tightly grasp yours,
for soon they will search
for new directions in which to grasp.
Cherish the growth —
the first step, smile, and word —
for soon they will
make way for new accomplishments.
Cherish with patience and love
each day with your children set before you,
because soon they become
memories to be tucked away.
Love with all your heart
the blessed gift of your child
and appreciate each and every moment.

Katherine J. Romboldi

ACKNOWLEDGMENTS

We gratefully acknowledge the permission granted by the following authors, publishers, and authors' representatives to reprint poems or excerpts from their publications.

HarperCollins Publishers, Inc., for "It is beautiful..." by Mother Teresa from MY LIFE FOR THE POOR, edited by José Luis González-Balado and Janet N. Playfoot. Copyright © 1985 by José Luis González-Balado and Janet N. Playfoot. And for "Accept your children...," "Children raised...," and "Hold them..." from WHAT DO YOU REALLY WANT FOR YOUR CHILDREN? by Dr. Wayne W. Dyer. Copyright © 1985 by Dr. Wayne W. Dyer. And for "Five Keys to Using Encouragement," Childhood is a time...," "Conveying our love...," and "The Nine Basic Ingredients for Falling in Love with Your Kids" from THE MAGIC OF ENCOURAGEMENT by Stephanie Marston. Copyright © 1990 by Stephanie Marston. And for "It must have been..." from THE IRRATIONAL SEASON by Madeleine L'Engle. Copyright © 1977 by Crosswicks, Ltd. And for "How can you explain..." from BABYHOOD by Paul Reiser. Copyright © 1997 by Paul Reiser. And for "In reality..." from GOLDEN RULES by Wayne Dosick. Copyright © 1995 by Wayne Dosick. All rights reserved.

Dutton, a division of Penguin Putnam Inc., for "Taking care of their children..." and "All parents expect..." from DR. SPOCK'S BABY AND CHILD CARE by Benjamin Spock, M.D., and Michael B. Rothenberg, M.D. Copyright © 1992 by Benjamin Spock, M.D. All rights reserved.

Celestial Arts for "Raising healthy children..." and "Kids are a great excuse..." from THE WINNING FAMILY by Dr. Louise Hart. Copyright © 1987, 1990, 1993 by Louise Hart. Celestial Arts, P.O. Box 7123, Berkeley, CA 94707. All rights reserved.

Karen M. Talmo for "As You Enter the Awesome Role of Parenthood" and "You Are Not Alone." Copyright © 2000 by Karen M. Talmo. All rights reserved.

Viking Penguin, a division of Penguin Putnam Inc., for "For all parents..." and "... a complex thing..." from YOU ARE SPECIAL by Fred Rogers. Copyright © 1994 by Family Communications, Inc. All rights reserved.

Harmony Books, a division of The Crown Publishing Group, for "The earlier someone is taught..." and "Remember that children..." from THE SEVEN SPIRITUAL LAWS FOR PARENTS by Deepak Chopra. Copyright © 1997 by Deepak Chopra, M.D. All rights reserved.

St. Martin's Press for "Time is the most valuable..." from IT TAKES A PARENT TO RAISE A CHILD by Glen C. Griffin, M.D., published by Golden Books. Copyright © 1999 by Dr. Glen C. Griffin. All rights reserved.

Bobbie Sandoz for "The gift of time...," "The greatest parenting challenge...," "The primary key...," and "Each time we..." from PARACHUTES FOR PARENTS by Bobbie Sandoz, published by Family Works Publications. Copyright © 1997 by Bobbie Sandoz. All rights reserved.

Jason Aronson, Inc., for "One of the greatest gifts...," "...not a natural ability...," and "To be a good parent..." from HOW TO INFLUENCE CHILDREN by Charles E. Schaefer, Ph.D. Copyright © 1982 by Van Nostrand Reinhold Company, Inc. All rights reserved.

Ellen Walker for "Children provide parents..." from GROWING UP WITH MY CHILDREN by Ellen Walker, published by Hazelden Foundation. Copyright © 1988 by Hazelden Foundation. All rights reserved.

Harcourt, Inc., for "Grown-ups never..." from THE LITTLE PRINCE by Antoine de Saint-Exupéry. Copyright © 1943, renewed 1971 by Harcourt, Inc. All rights reserved.

Doubleday, a division of Random House, Inc., for "Children are adoring..." from GROWING UP HAPPY by Bob Keeshan. Copyright © 1989 by Bob Keeshan. All rights reserved.

Tom Ryan for "A Small Child." Copyright © 2000 by Tom Ryan. All rights reserved.

Bloch Publishing Company for "Parents are in..." from WHEN YOUR CHILD ASKS: A HANDBOOK FOR JEWISH PARENTS by Simon Glustrom. Copyright © 1991 by Simon Glustrom. All rights reserved.

Putnam Berkley, a division of Penguin Putnam Inc., for "Children are naturally..." and "Kids love to feel..." from 150 WAYS TO HELP YOUR CHILD SUCCEED by Karin Ireland. Copyright © 1998 by Karin Ireland. All rights reserved.

Simon & Schuster for "Role modeling is..." from PRINCIPLE-CENTERED LEADERSHIP by Stephen R. Covey. Copyright © 1990, 1991 by Stephen R. Covey. And for "Parents bear the first..." from IT TAKES A VILLAGE by Hillary Rodham Clinton. Copyright © 1996 by Hillary Rodham Clinton. And for "Some people think..." from DR. SPOCK ON PARENTING by Benjamin Spock, M.D. Copyright © 1988 by Benjamin Spock. All rights reserved.

Scholastic Inc. for "Children watch the way..." from COLIN POWELL: A BIOGRAPHY BY JIM HASKINS. Copyright © 1992 by James Haskins. All rights reserved.

Barbara Cage for "...touches that bond..." Copyright © 2000 by Barbara Cage. All rights reserved.

Conari Press for "...gifts from God...," "...a blessing...," "Parenting is hard...," and "A nurturing home..." from WONDERFUL WAYS TO LOVE A CHILD by Judy Ford. Copyright © 1995 by Judy Ford. All rights reserved.

Linda LaBella-Morgan for "Children Are Angels Who Walk the Earth." Copyright © 2000 by Linda LaBella-Morgan. All rights reserved.

Workman Publishing Company, Inc., for "The root meaning..." from CHILDREN LEARN WHAT THEY LIVE by Dorothy Law Nolte and Rachel Harris. Copyright © 1998 by Dorothy Law Nolte and Rachel Harris. All rights reserved.

Prentice-Hall, Inc., Upper Saddle River, NJ, for "Children need encouragement..." from ENCOURAGING CHILDREN TO LEARN by Rudolph Dreikurs. Copyright © 1964 by Rudolph Dreikurs. All rights reserved.

Regnery Publishing, Inc., for "In every place..." and "I think that..." from COLLECTED VERSE OF EDGAR A. GUEST. Copyright © 1934 by Regnery Publishing. All rights reserved.

Bantam Books, a division of Random House, Inc., for "Obviously, it would be ludicrous..." from LOVING EACH ONE BEST by Nancy Samalin. Copyright © 1996 by Nancy Samalin. And for "The only rock..." from TALKING STRAIGHT by Lee Iacocca. Copyright © 1988 by Lee Iacocca. All rights reserved.

Craig Chappelow for "Do not underestimate...." Copyright © 2000 by Craig Chappelow. All rights reserved.

M. Joye for "A father is a guide...." Copyright © 2000 by M. Joye. All rights reserved.

Hugh Prather for "Take this still..." from NOTES ON HOW TO LIVE IN THE WORLD AND STILL BE HAPPY by Hugh Prather, published by Doubleday, a division of Random House, Inc. Copyright © 1986 by Hugh Prather. All rights reserved.

Deanna Beisser for "Before I leave this world..." from IS IT TIME TO MAKE A CHANGE?, published by SPS Studios, Inc. Copyright © 1997 by Deanna Beisser. All rights reserved.

Alfred A. Knopf, a division of Random House, Inc., for "Parents' Creed" from THE PROPHET by Kahlil Gibran. Copyright © 1923 by Kahlil Gibran, renewal copyright 1951 by Administrators C.T.A. of Kahlil Gibran Estate and Mary G. Gibran. All rights reserved.

The Trustees of Mrs. F. C. Cornford, Cambridge, England, for "They must go free..." from "Ode of the Whole Duty of Parents" by Frances Crofts Cornford. Published 1934 by Cambridge University Press.

Katherine J. Romboldi for "Hold close to your heart...." Copyright © 2000 by Katherine J. Romboldi. All rights reserved.

A careful effort has been made to trace the ownership of selections used in this anthology in order to obtain permission to reprint copyrighted materials and give proper credit to the copyright owners. If any error or omission has occurred, it is completely inadvertent, and we would like to make corrections in future editions provided that written notification is made to the publisher:

SPS STUDIOS, INC., P.O. Box 4549, Boulder, Colorado 80306.

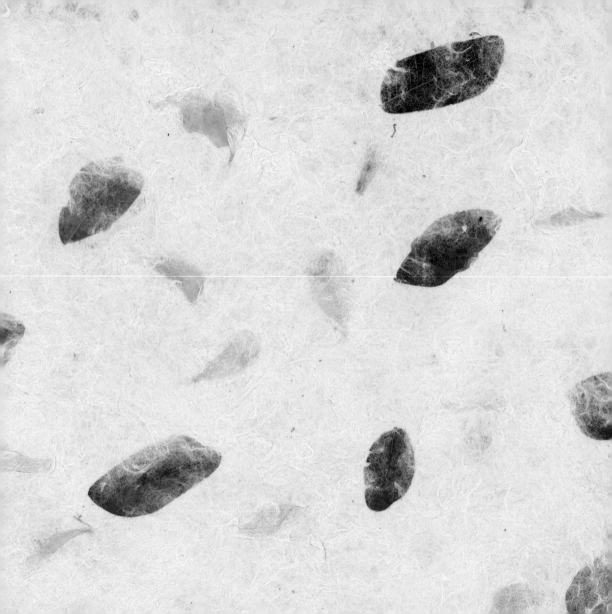